Building Essential Language Arts Skills

GRADE 3

New York • Toronto • London • Auckland • Sydney
Mexico City • New Delhi • Hong Kong • Buenos Aires

Writer: Tina Posner
Editors: Maria L. Chang, Chris Bennett
Cover design: Tannaz Fassihi; Cover art: Ana Bermejo
Interior design: Shekhar Kapur, Michelle H. Kim; Interior art: QBS Learning
Produced with QBS Learning

ISBN: 978-0-545-85035-3
Copyright © 2016 by Scholastic Inc.
All rights reserved. Printed in the U.S.A.
First printing, June 2016.

1 2 3 4 5 6 7 8 9 10   40   22 21 20 19 18 17 16

Table of Contents

Introduction

Help students master key language arts skills with this standards-based workbook, designed to help them become successful readers and writers. Fun and engaging reproducible activity pages provide targeted practice on important skills and concepts, such as parts of speech, capitalization, punctuation, spelling, vocabulary, and so much more.

The ready-to-go practice pages in *Building Essential Language Arts Skills* are versatile and can be used in different ways:

- Select a skills page and use it as a "do now" activity to help students get settled first thing in the morning. Simply stack copies of the page on your desk for students to pick up as they enter the room and give the class five minutes to complete the activity.

- Preview the day's lesson with an appropriate skills page to find out what students already know about the topic.

- Alternatively, you can also use a skills page to review a recent lesson and assess what students have learned and what still needs further instruction.

- Assign pages for homework or independent work as needed.

An answer key is provided at the back of the book so you can review answers with the whole class. In doing so, you provide students with opportunities for discussion, reinforcement, or extension to other lessons. You may also want to encourage students to discuss their answers and strategies in small groups. This collaboration enables students to deepen their understanding or clarify any misunderstandings they may have about the skill or concept.

Meeting the Common Core State Standards

The activities in this workbook meet the following Common Core State Standards for English Language Arts. For more information about the standards, go to http://www.corestandards.org/ELA-Literacy.

Grade 3 Language Skills

L.3.1.a Explain the function of nouns, pronouns, verbs, adjectives, and adverbs in general and their functions in particular sentences.

L.3.1.b Form and use regular and irregular plural nouns.

L.3.1.c Use abstract nouns.

L.3.1.d Form and use regular and irregular verbs.

L.3.1.e Form and use the simple verb tenses.

L.3.1.f Ensure subject-verb and pronoun-antecedent agreement.

L.3.1.g Form and use comparative and superlative adjectives and adverbs, and choose between them depending on what is to be modified.

L.3.1.h Use coordinating and subordinating conjunctions.

L.3.1.i Produce simple, compound, and complex sentences.

L.3.2.a Capitalize appropriate words in titles.

L.3.2.b Use commas in addresses.

L.3.2.c Use commas and quotation marks in dialogue.

L.3.2.d Form and use possessives.

L.3.2.e Use conventional spelling for high-frequency and other studied words and for adding suffixes to base words.

L.3.2.f Use spelling patterns and generalizations (e.g., word families, position-based spellings, syllable patterns, ending rules, meaningful word parts) in writing words.

L.3.3.a Choose words and phrases for effect.

L.3.3.b Recognize and observe differences between the conventions of spoken and written standard English.

L.3.4.a Use sentence-level context as a clue to the meaning of a word or phrase.

L.3.4.b Determine the meaning of the new word formed when a known affix is added to a known word.

L.3.4.c Use a known root word as a clue to the meaning of an unknown word with the same root.

L.3.5.a Distinguish the literal and nonliteral meanings of words and phrases in context.

L.3.5.b Identify real-life connections between words and their use.

L.3.5.c Distinguish shades of meaning among related words that describe states of mind or degrees of certainty.

L.3.6 Acquire and use accurately grade-appropriate conversational, general academic, and domain-specific words and phrases, including those that signal spatial and temporal relationships.

A **noun** names a person, place, or thing.
A **proper noun** names a specific person, place, or thing. It always begins with a capital letter.
For example, *teacher* is a common noun, and *Mr. Roberts* is a proper noun.

Nouns Around Town

Write *person*, *place*, or *thing* to describe each picture.
Then write a noun that names the picture.

1. _____   2. _____   3. _____

_____   _____   _____

Underline the common nouns in each sentence. Circle the proper nouns.

4. Duke is a big white dog.

5. This dog was elected mayor of Cormorant.

6. Cormorant is a very small town in Minnesota.

7. The town is full of dogs like Duke,
   but only one person lives there.

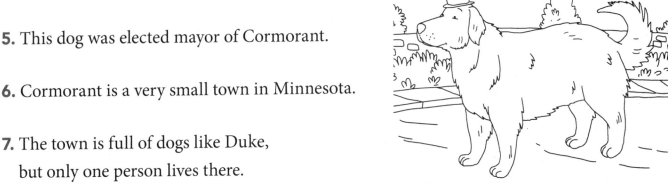

8. That person is Dolores Cormorant, a big dog lover.

Building Essential Language Arts Skills: Grade 3 © Scholastic Inc.

Name: _____   Date: _____

If a noun ends in *-s, -sh, -ch, -x,* or *-z,* add *-es* to make it plural. For example, *buses, inches,* and *taxes.*

From Fox to Foxes

Fill in the blanks to make these nouns plural.

1. The two fox_____ hid in the box_____.

2. They had bunch_____ of grapes in their lunch_____.

3. They ate them quietly in the bush_____.

Write the plural noun for each picture.

4.

_____

5.

_____

6.

_____

Building Essential Language Arts Skills: Grade 3 © Scholastic Inc.

To make a word that ends in *y* plural, change the *y* to *i* and add *-es* (as in the word *cities*). But if the word ends in a vowel +*y*, just add *-s* (as in *cowboys*).

The Changing Y

Write the plural noun for each picture.

1. _____   2. _____   3. _____

Pick a noun from the box to fill in each blank. Make the noun plural.

> bunny   puppy   monkey   hobby   berry

4. The _____ at the zoo are funny.

5. What are your favorite _____?

6. Ana's dog gave birth to several _____.

7. The cowboy loves to eat _____.

8. The _____ hopped around the park.

Building Essential Language Arts Skills: Grade 3 © Scholastic Inc.

Name: _____   Date: _____

Falling Leaf to Leaves

Write the plural of each noun.

1. life _____

3. wolf _____

2. loaf _____

4. cliff _____

Fill in the blanks by making the words plural. The first one is done for you.

The tree in Owen's yard lost all of its _____leaves_____ *(leaf)* in the fall. He and

his sister had to rake the yard. Before they went outside, they put on their

_____ *(scarf)*. Then, they went out and split the yard into

two _____ *(half)*. They each raked their half.

Name: _____ Date: _____

  Some plural nouns don't end in *s* or *es*. They have different spellings from their singular versions, such as the words *mouse* and *mice*. Other nouns, like *moose*, do not change when they are plural.

Mouse or Mice?

Make each noun plural.
Then find the plural nouns in the word search.

1. goose _____

2. woman _____

3. child _____

4. foot _____

5. sheep _____

6. deer _____

7. cactus _____

8. tooth _____

C	S	C	A	C	T	I	S	I
H	T	W	S	L	D	E	E	R
I	G	Z	W	F	R	H	L	H
L	S	F	O	L	I	V	L	H
D	H	F	M	F	O	L	Z	X
R	E	T	E	E	T	H	Q	Z
E	E	O	N	E	A	X	Q	N
N	P	Y	D	T	M	I	C	F
V	G	E	E	S	E	U	K	P

Name: _____ Date: _____

 Concrete nouns name things you can touch or see, such as *book* and *tree*.
Abstract nouns name ideas, such as *happiness* and *love*.

You Can't Touch This!

Look at the words in the box. Write the concrete nouns under the picture of the rock.
Write the abstract nouns under the cloud.

childhood	pencil	freedom	president
water	fear	calendar	friendship

Concrete Nouns

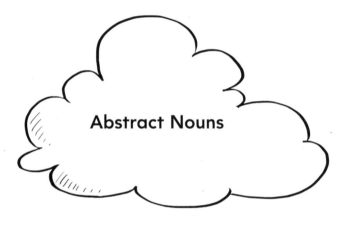

Abstract Nouns

_____   _____

_____   _____

_____   _____

_____   _____

Building Essential Language Arts Skills: Grade 3 © Scholastic Inc.

A **pronoun** takes the place of a noun in a sentence.
Make sure pronouns match the nouns they replace.
For example, the plural noun *children* should be replaced by the plural pronoun *they* or *them*.

The Bear Is It

Fill in each sentence with a pronoun from the box. Circle the word that the pronoun needs to match. The first one has been done for you.

> it   he   we   his   her   them

1. Charlie's (bear) was lost, but I found it __it__ .

2. Amy lost _____ favorite ring.

3. Kevin spilled juice on _____ shirt.

4. Our family wants a new TV, so _____ are going shopping.

5. The teacher called Jon to see if _____ was feeling better.

6. Paul and Matt will be late, so we'll start without _____ .

Name: _____   Date: _____

 Use singular pronouns to replace singular nouns and plural pronouns to replace plural nouns. For example, replace *sweater* with *it* and *mittens* with *them*.

Does This Pronoun Match?

Look at the underlined pronoun. Then circle what it stands for.

1. Kevin wore his favorite shorts even though <u>they</u> didn't match his jacket.

2. Tony and Frank saw it was raining, so <u>they</u> took umbrellas to school.

3. My brother and I ran home because <u>we</u> didn't have coats.

Write a pronoun that makes sense in the sentences.

4. I know the shoes fit because I tried _____ on.

5. Tom's clothes are wet because _____ was caught in a storm.

6. I put my hat away, but now I can't find _____.

A **verb** shows action. It can be one word or it can include a helping verb, such as _is running_ or _are reading_.
For example, in the sentence "I am going to the store," _am going_ is the complete verb.

Action!

Circle the complete verb in each sentence.

1. The hero fell from a window.

2. But he landed on a mattress.

3. He was running away from the bad guys.

4. They are chasing him.

5. A big fight scene is coming up!

Complete each sentence. Use a helping verb at least once.

6. In some movies, cars

_____.

7. People who drive these cars

_____.

8. In a movie, I would like to see a car

_____.

Name: _____ Date: _____

 Most verbs form their **past tense** by adding *-ed*, or just *-d* if the word already ends in *-e*.
For words like *cry*, change the *y* to *i* and then add *-ed* (*cried*).
For words that end with a short vowel sound, like *hop*,
double the last letter and then add *-ed* (*hopped*).

The Past Ends in -ed

Write the past tense form of each verb.

1. Kelly _____ *(start)* with the number 10.

2. Next, she _____ *(add)* 6 and then _____ *(divide)* by 2.

3. Then she _____ *(subtract)* 3 from the number.

4. After she _____ *(multiply)* by 2, she _____ *(end)*

up with the same number!

Rewrite the sentences using the past tense of the verbs.

5. Ed and Ted walk and talk about old times.

_____

6. They wave to other friends in the park.

_____

7. Then the two of them play cards.

_____

8. After that, they hurry to catch a bus home.

_____

Building Essential Language Arts Skills: Grade 3 © Scholastic Inc.

Name: _____ Date: _____

We Drove to the Drive-In

bring   take

go   eat

drink   build

Complete the sentences with the past tense of one of the verbs above.

1. The owners _____ this drive-in movie theater in 1956.

2. Last night we _____ to see a science-fiction movie there.

3. We _____ snacks from home to eat.

4. I _____ some orange juice.

5. My sister _____ my popcorn when I wasn't looking.

6. So I _____ some of her candy.

Some verbs are irregular in the past tense. Irregular verbs change spelling in different ways, such as *eat/ate* or *stand/stood*.

It's in the Past

Write a sentence about each picture. Use the verb in bold.
Make sure the verb is in the past tense.

1.   **swim**   _____

_____

2.   **write**   _____

_____

3.   **dig**   _____

_____

4.   **sleep**   _____

_____

Building Essential Language Arts Skills: Grade 3 © Scholastic Inc.

Name: _____   Date: _____

 To make the **future tense** of a verb, add the helping verb *will* to a verb in the present tense. For example: *I will travel to the future in my time machine.*

You Will Time Travel

Choose a verb from the box and fill in the blanks to make the future tense. The first one has been done for you.

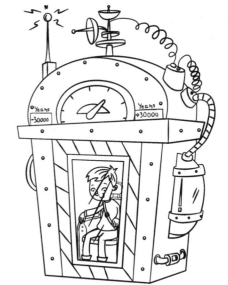

| travel | happen | drive | eat |
| wake up | get | take | |

1. Randall knows what ___will happen___ tomorrow.

2. He _____ pancakes for breakfast.

3. He _____ late and miss the bus to school.

4. His father _____ him to school.

5. He _____ a spelling test.

6. He _____ all the words right!

7. He _____ back from the future in time to wake up today!

Write two sentences about what you will do tomorrow.
Make sure to use verbs in the future tense.

Tomorrow, I _____

_____

_____

> Use a singular verb with a singular subject. Use a plural verb with a plural subject. For example: *Cherries taste* delicious. A *cherry* on a hot dog *tastes* gross!

Do These Go Together?

Underline the subject of the sentence. Then write the verb that agrees with it.

1. The dogs that live next door _____ all night long. (*bark, barks*)

2. The stars _____ in the night sky. (*sparkles, sparkle*)

3. A squirrel _____ at the feeder hanging on the porch. (*nibbles, nibble*)

4. The sun _____ through the window. (*shine, shines*)

5. The cat sitting on the books _____ to sleep in the sun. (*love, loves*)

6. Snow and ice _____ slippery roads. (*cause, causes*)

7. The leaves on the oak tree _____ to the ground. (*falls, fall*)

Building Essential Language Arts Skills: Grade 3 © Scholastic Inc.

An **adjective** describes a noun or pronoun.
If you say, "the red house," the word *red* is an adjective that describes *house*.

A Tasty Feast

Circle the adjectives in each sentence.

1. Dad wore an ugly brown sweater.

2. Grandpa served the juicy meat.

3. After dinner, I had a full stomach.

Write two adjectives to describe each noun.
Then write a sentence using the adjectives and noun.

4. _____ _____ turkey

_____

5. _____ _____ vegetables

_____

6. _____ _____ potatoes

_____

7. _____ _____ pie

_____

Name: _____ Date: _____

When comparing two things, add *-er* to an adjective *(faster)*.
For words that end in *-y*, change the *y* to *i*, then add *-er*.
If the adjective has more than two syllables, use the word *more* instead *(more difficult)*.

Comparing Apples and Oranges

Use the *-er* ending or the word *more*.

1. nice _____

2. exciting _____

3. important _____

4. happy _____

Complete the sentences using the adjective given at the end.
Add *-er* to the adjective or use the word *more*.

5. Oranges are _____ *(juicy)* than apples.

6. Oranges have to be peeled, so they are _____

 (difficult) to eat than apples.

7. Oranges are _____ *(round)* than apples,

 so they are perfect for juggling!

8. Apples make a _____ *(delicious)* pie

 than oranges!

Building Essential Language Arts Skills: Grade 3 © Scholastic Inc.

Name: _____ Date: _____

> To compare three or more things, add -est to an adjective *(hardest)*.
> For words that end in -y, change the *y* to *i*, then add -est.
> Use the word *most* with adjectives that have two or more syllables *(most colorful)*.

The Toast With the Most

Use the -est ending or the word *most* with each of these words.

1. kind _____

2. beautiful _____

3. intelligent _____

4. funny _____

Add -est to the adjectives shown or use the word *most*.
Then finish these compliments with your own ideas.

5. The _____ *(helpful)* person I know is _____.

6. The _____ *(tasty)* food I have ever eaten is _____.

7. The _____ *(nice)* person in my class is _____.

8. The _____ *(interesting)* movie I've seen is

_____.

Building Essential Language Arts Skills: Grade 3 © Scholastic Inc.

Adverbs tell how, when, or where something happens. If you say, "I'll return here soon," *here* and *soon* are adverbs that tell where and when you'll return.

Too Warm Too Quickly

Write whether each adverb tells *how*, *when*, or *where*.

1. later _____

2. carefully _____

3. there _____

4. excitedly _____

5. yesterday _____

6. inside _____

Underline the two adverbs in each sentence.

7. The sun glistened brightly and slowly melted the snowman.

8. I'll go outside tomorrow when it is warmer.

Add an adverb to each sentence.

9. We went for a walk _____ the storm.

10. We walked _____ through the streets.

Name: _____ Date: _____

Conjunctions such as *and*, *but*, and *or* can be used to join two or more items. For example: *I like chocolate <u>and</u> vanilla ice cream.*

Stuck Together Like Glue

Join each sentence with a conjunction (*and*, *but*, *or*).

1. Do you ride the bus  walk to school?

2. Jon plays checkers  not chess.

3. Hannah likes to write poems  stories.

4. Grace is a good baseball player because she can hit  throw well.

5. Put on gloves  mittens if your hands are cold.

6. I like vanilla ice cream  not vanilla pudding.

Building Essential Language Arts Skills: Grade 3 © Scholastic Inc.

A **subordinating conjunction** introduces a group of words, or a clause, that cannot stand alone. For example: *I will clean my bedroom <u>when</u> I get home from school.*

Make a Clean Connection

Draw a line to match the sentence parts that go together.
One part should have an underlined subordinating conjunction.
The first one has been done for you.

 1. <u>Although</u> I cleaned last week,   <u>so</u> I can use it for school tomorrow.

 2. My clothes are all wrinkled   I will put them away.

 3. <u>After</u> I fold my clothes,   my room is messy again.

 4. I can listen to some music   <u>because</u> I left them on the floor.

 5. I need to find my backpack   I need to clear off my bed.

 **6.** <u>Before</u> I go to sleep,   <u>while</u> I clean my room.

Building Essential Language Arts Skills: Grade 3 © Scholastic Inc.

Name: _____   Date: _____

 Combine two sentences by adding a comma and a conjunction between them. Choose a conjunction such as *and, but, or,* or *so.*

Strange Combinations

Pablo Pistachio is a talented artist known for his animal drawings. He likes to combine animals in strange ways. Read the sentences below. Combine the two sentences using a comma and conjunction *(and, so, but, or).*

1. Pablo Pistachio gave the rat wings. It looked pleased.

_____

2. Pablo likes butterflies. He decided to combine one with a fish.

_____

3. Pablo put a turtle's shell on a duck. He put a duck's bill on a turtle.

_____

4. He could give the raccoon a camel's hump. He could give it a lion's face.

_____

5. The giraffe looked good with feathers. The hippo did not.

_____

More Strange Combinations

Pablo Pistachio is at it again. Cross out the incorrect conjunction in each sentence and write the correct one.

1. Pablo almost put a pig's snout on a Cheshire cat, so it didn't look right.

_____

2. An Asian elephant had a cheetah's legs, or it could run faster.

_____

3. I see a buffalo head on a rhino, but it looks friendly.

_____

4. Do not copy one of Pablo's drawings, and he might get mad.

_____

Write two compound sentences about your own ideas for a weird animal drawing. Don't forget to use a conjunction in each sentence.

5. _____

6. _____

Building Essential Language Arts Skills: Grade 2 © Scholastic Inc.

Name: _____ Date: _____

Put a Tail on Your Tale

Extend each sentence using the word in parentheses.
The first one has been done for you.

1. We will eat the birthday cake. *(after)*

We will eat the birthday cake after we open the presents.

2. I got a stomachache. *(because)*

_____

3. The kids played games. *(before)*

_____

4. They took turns whacking the piñata. *(until)*

_____

5. We'll go out for pizza. *(when)*

_____

6. We sang in the car. *(while)*

_____

Name: _____   Date: _____

Name Calling

Write the title of your favorite book, TV show, and movie.

If you don't have a favorite, you can make one up.

1.  _____

2.  _____

3.  _____

Draw three lines under each letter that should be capitalized in these titles.
The first one is done for you.

4. march of the penguins

5. casey at the bat

6. cloudy with a chance of meatballs

7. tales of a fourth grade nothing

Name: _____ Date: _____

 When you write an address on one line, put a comma between the street name and the city. Always put a comma between the city and the state.
For example: *Last year we visited Miami, Florida.*

Special Delivery

Put commas where they belong.

1. Mr. Jack Frost lives at 1000 Cold Street Burrville Alaska.

2. Ms. Anita Mittens lives at 345 Flake Lane Snowtown New York.

Fill in this envelope from Jack Frost to Anita Mittens.

_____

_____

_____

99501

_____

_____

_____

11901

Name: _____ Date: _____

Put commas between the name of a city and state or country.
Put another comma after the state or country if the sentence continues.
For example: *My cousin went to Paris, France, with her high school class.*

Going Global

Deliver the commas to the correct places.

1. Paul   wants   to   visit   Paris   France.

2. Have   you   ever   been   to   Cheyenne   Wyoming?

3. We   had   fun   visiting   Toronto   Canada   last   year.

4. Egon   moved   here   from   Budapest   Hungary.

5. Austin   Texas   gets   very   hot   in   the   summer.

6. San   Francisco   California   can   be   very   foggy.

Name: _____   Date: _____

 Use quotation marks around the exact words that someone said.
Use a comma to separate the quoted words from the rest of the sentence.
For example: *Sonia said, "Hi!"*

Punctuation Parachutes

Drop the correct punctuation into the sentences below. The first one has been done for you.

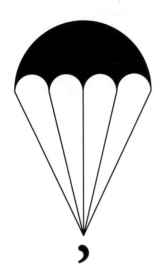 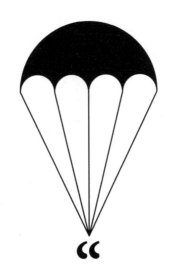 

,   **"**   **"**

1. Ms. Taylor said**,**   "I'm your new teacher."

2. Frank   said   I   want   to   read   a   book   about   explorers.

3. My   sister   asked   What   movie   do   you   want   to   see?

4. Jim   shouted   Shoot   the   ball!

5. I   heard   a   strange   noise   Lisa   whispered.

6. Cary   mumbled   I   forgot   my   math   homework.

7. You   need   to   rake   the   leaves   said   Dad.

If a quote contains a question mark or exclamation point, you do not need a comma. For example: *"Hi, Sonia!" yelled Paul.*

Comic Quotation

Write the dialogue from the comic strip. Add commas and quotation marks to show what Josh and Mom say.

1. Josh said _____

2. Mom asked _____

3. _____ Josh replied.

4. _____ offered Mom.

5. Josh said _____.

6. _____ Mom said.

To show that a person or thing owns something, add an apostrophe and an *s*. For example: *bird's cage* or *Marcel's pencil*

The Cat's Meow

Write the possessive form of the underlined words.

1. The collar belongs to the <u>cat</u>. It's the _____ collar.

2. The mane belongs to the <u>horse</u>. It's the _____ mane.

3. The saddle belongs to <u>Tom</u>. It's _____ saddle.

4. The books belong to the <u>school</u>. They're the _____ books.

5. I saw a cute <u>kitten</u>. The _____ tail was fluffy.

6. The kitten chewed the <u>toy</u>. The _____ stuffing was everywhere!

7. I also saw a <u>turtle</u>. The _____ shell was brown and gold.

Name: _____ Date: _____

The Bees' Knees

Write the possessive form of the underlined words.

1. Sarah and Vicky raise <u>bees</u>. The _____ honey is delicious.

2. Bees help <u>farmers</u>. They help the _____ crops.

3. Look at the wheels on the <u>cars</u>. The _____ wheels are flat.

4. Where are the supplies for the <u>students</u>? The _____ supplies are in the closet.

5. I found the den that the <u>foxes</u> live in. The _____ den is near the river.

6. Have you visited the coop where the <u>chickens</u> lay their eggs? The _____ coop is next to the barn.

Name: _____ Date: _____

 Some words change spelling when you add an ending, such as *-ing* or *-ed*.
Drop the final *-e* before adding *-ing* (*leaving*). Change the final *-y* to *i* before adding *-ed* (*tried*).

All's Well That Ends Well

Fill in the blank with the correct form of the verb in parentheses.
Add *-ed* or *-ing* and change the spelling as needed.

1. Long ago, pirates _____ *(bury)* a treasure chest on an island.

2. They never came back for it, so it _____ *(stay)* there.

3. Miguel and Kathy _____ *(try)* to find the treasure.

4. They were _____ *(hope)* an old map would lead them to it.

5. They saw something that was _____ *(cover)* by the sand.

6. They both _____ *(smile)* because they had found the treasure!

Building Essential Language Arts Skills: Grade 3 © Scholastic Inc.

Name: _____ Date: _____

If a word ends with a short vowel sound, double the last consonant before you add an ending, such as *-ed* or *-ing*. For example: *cut/cutting*

The Recipe for Doubling

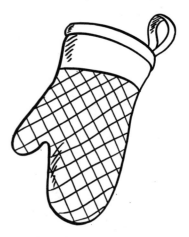

Fill in the empty boxes of the chart. Listen to the vowel sound in each word. Then decide if you need to double the last letter before you add the ending.

base word	add -ed	add -ing
chop		
flip		
boil		
drain		
whip		

Write your own sentence about cooking, using at least two of the words above.

_____

_____

Building Essential Language Arts Skills: Grade 3 © Scholastic Inc.

Name: _____   Date: _____

 Some words have silent letters, such as the *b* in *thumb*, the *k* in *knit*, the *w* in *wrong*, the *gh* in *light*, the *n* in *column*, and the *l* in *walk*.

Do Gnomes Knit?

Read the clues. Then fill in the missing letters.

1. A sharp tool for cutting

2. The season that comes after summer

3. To go up, as in a tree

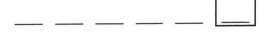

4. To hear

5. The opposite of right

6. The thing on the corner that tells the street's name

7. Where a king or queen lives

Write the letters in the boxes to answer the question.

What do you call a funny gnome who knits?

A __ __ __ __ __   __ __ __ !

The /f/ sound can be spelled with *f*, *ff*, *gh*, or *ph*.
For example: *fun, puff, cough,* and *elephant*

Can an Elephant Laugh?

Replace the misspelled word in parentheses with the correctly spelled word.

1. Use a camera to take a _____ *(fotograf)* of the smiling elephant.

2. Something funny must have made the elephant _____ *(laf)*.

3. Maybe the elephant isn't smiling, but has a cold and is _____ *(coffing)*.

4. The opposite of smooth is _____ *(ruph)*.

5. If you try hard to play the saxophone, you show _____ *(ephort)*.

6. You can put your books and folders on the _____ *(shelph)*.

7. The ABCs are also called the _____ *(alfabet)*.

Name: _____ Date: _____

Shriek! Is It *Ei* or *Ie*?

Spell the words in parentheses correctly. Hint: Read the words aloud to help you.

1. _____ *(Feeld)* mouse Franny saw something she had never seen before.

2. Spider Stan fell off the _____ *(seeling)* and landed on the floor.

He too had not seen such a thing before.

3. It had green skin, big purple lips, and _____ *(ate)* arms.

4. Its _____ *(hite)* was about three feet above the door.

5. Oh, it is just Mrs. Ford's _____ *(naybor)*, Eddie the alien.

6. He is the _____ *(phrendly)* new _____ *(casheer)* at the store.

Name: _____ Date: _____

 A **prefix** is a word part added to the beginning of a word root.
The prefixes *un-*, *im-*, and *dis-* mean "not," as in *unhappy*, *impossible*, and *disrespectful*.
The prefix *re-* means "again," as in <u>*reread*</u>.
The prefix *pre-* means "before," as in <u>*preheat*</u>.

Find the Prefix

Write the prefix word based on the definition.
Then help Harry Hound find the words in the puzzle.

1. to view before _____

2. not polite _____

3. to not like _____

4. to build again _____

5. not able _____

C	K	E	I	I	E	U	P	E	T
R	U	W	M	S	J	O	R	K	K
U	N	X	P	G	C	W	E	J	Q
Z	A	K	O	Z	S	H	V	C	V
D	B	L	L	V	W	V	I	A	A
Q	L	K	I	J	N	N	E	N	E
G	E	Z	T	K	H	K	W	D	P
L	S	E	E	T	I	L	D	Z	N
D	I	S	L	I	K	E	A	E	A
U	D	R	E	B	U	I	L	D	R

Building Essential Language Arts Skills: Grade 3 © Scholastic Inc.

Name: _____ Date: _____

 A **suffix** is a word part added to the end of a word root.
The ending -*ful* means "full of," as in *hopeful*.
The ending -*less* means "without," as in *fearless*.
The ending -*er* means "someone who does that," as in *baker*.

Serving Up Suffixes

Use a suffix to complete each word.

1. Todd taught his students to cook. He was a good teach_____.

2. Delia cleaned up after the cooking class. She was very help_____.

3. Jerald's muffins had no taste. They were flavor_____.

Write another word with each suffix. Then write what that word means.

4. _____ful   means   _____

5. _____less   means   _____

6. _____er   means   _____

Name: _____ Date: _____

 Each **syllable** in a word makes one vowel sound.
For example, the word *animal* has three vowel sounds and three syllables: an • i • mal.

Animal Sounds

Count the syllables in each word and sort the animals where they belong.
Write another animal name on the third line in each syllable group.

deer	lion	rhinoceros	butterfly
monkey	goat	elephant	alligator

1 Syllable

1. _____

2. _____

3. _____

2 Syllables

4. _____

5. _____

6. _____

3 Syllables

7. _____

8. _____

9. _____

4 Syllables

10. _____

11. _____

12. _____

Building Essential Language Arts Skills: Grade 3 © Scholastic Inc.

Name: _____   Date: _____

 To put words in ABC order, compare the first letters. If they are the same, go on to the second letter, and then to the third and fourth letters if you need to.

The Alphabet Parade

1. Rewrite these words in alphabetical order. The first word has been written for you.

candy   _____ant_____

kind   _____

ant   _____

nose   _____

tiny   _____

2. Now rewrite these words in alphabetical order.

lazy   _____

lead   _____

laugh   _____

law   _____

laundry   _____

3. Think of a word that could be the last word in each list.

List 1: _____

List 2: _____

Name: _____   Date: _____

Go With a Guide

Look at the guide words for each dictionary page. Put a check mark next to the words that you can find on that page.

1. dream • drive

drum _____

dress _____

dragon _____

drink _____

draw _____

2. home • honk

honey _____

homonym _____

holiday _____

honest _____

hockey _____

Write another word you could find between the guide words.

3. Between *dream* and *drive*: _____

4. Between *home* and *honk*: _____

Name: _____ Date: _____

 Choose specific words to make your writing livelier. For example: It's more specific to say *drizzling* or *pouring* than *raining*.

Spice It Up!

Rewrite these sentences to spice them up.
Replace each underlined word with a word from the box.

| spit | slid | sizzling |
| complained | squirting | |

1. Anna cracked some eggs into the <u>hot</u> frying pan.

_____

2. She <u>took</u> them out of the pan and served them to Matt.

_____

3. "Eggs are boring!" Matt <u>said</u>.

_____

4. "Try this," Anna said, <u>putting</u> some hot sauce on them.

_____

5. Matt <u>took</u> the food out of his mouth. "Too hot!" he cried.

_____

Building Essential Language Arts Skills: Grade 3 © Scholastic Inc.

Name: _____   Date: _____

 Informal English is fine when talking with friends.
When writing, use complete sentences and avoid using slang words.

Formal or Informal?

Read each sentence. Decide whether the language is written or spoken.
Check the correct box.

	Written	Spoken
1. That movie was awesome, right?	☐	☐
2. The actor gave a dramatic performance.	☐	☐
3. The storm deposited six inches of snow.	☐	☐
4. Hey, look at all that snow!	☐	☐
5. This new video game rocks.	☐	☐
6. This video game is easy to learn.	☐	☐

Howdy!

Good morning!

Building Essential Language Arts Skills: Grade 3 © Scholastic Inc.

If you don't know what a word means, think about the job it does in the sentence. Does it name something, describe something, or tell about an action?

Time for Context Clues

Read each sentence and look at the underlined word.
Decide what kind of word it is and circle the best answer.

1. Esteban and David set their alarm so they could <u>hustle</u> to the mall early.

    a. place   **b.** description   **c.** food   **d.** action

2. On the way to the mall, the bus stopped outside the <u>aquarium</u>.

    a. place   **b.** description   **c.** food   **d.** action

3. At the mall, David and Larry <u>browsed</u> the video games for over an hour.

    a. place   **b.** description   **c.** food   **d.** action

4. After that, they went to the food court for some <u>provisions</u>.

    a. place   **b.** description   **c.** food   **d.** action

5. The mall was <u>enormous</u>, so they had a long walk to catch the bus home.

    a. place   **b.** description   **c.** food   **d.** action

6. A lady carrying bags looked <u>exhausted</u>, so they let her sit down.

    a. place   **b.** description   **c.** food   **d.** action

Name: _____   Date: _____

 Look for clue words in a sentence to help you figure out the meaning of unfamiliar words.

Follow the Clues

Choose a definition for each underlined word. Use the clues
in bold to help you. Write the definition on the line below.

Definitions

very bad	great place	rested
tiring	very good	correctly

1. Our state has had <u>severe</u> weather with some **dangerous** storms.

_____

2. Bella had to **take a nap** after a <u>grueling</u> workout at the gym.

_____

3. The bird <u>perched</u> on the wire and **sat there** for a long time.

_____

4. Zach answered all the questions on his test <u>accurately</u> and had **no mistakes**.

_____

5. When Ellen stretched out on the **beach in the sun**, she felt she was in <u>paradise</u>.

_____

6. The **delicious pies** are just some of the treats at this <u>splendid</u> bakery.

_____

Building Essential Language Arts Skills: Grade 2 © Scholastic Inc.

Name: _____ Date: _____

 Use what you know about root words and prefixes to help you figure out the meaning of an unfamiliar word.
For example: *Unbendable* means "not able to bend."

Packing or Unpacking?

Complete the sentences with a word from the box that makes sense.

> unacceptable   disbelief   prepaid

1. We bought the train tickets last month so they were _____.

2. Mom looked at me in _____ when she could not lift my suitcase.

3. She said it was _____ for me to pack so many clothes!

Underline the prefix. Then draw a line to match the word with its meaning.

4. uncertain   not orderly

5. disorganized   to look at ahead of time

6. preview   not sure

Building Essential Language Arts Skills: Grade 3 © Scholastic Inc.

Name: _____ Date: _____

 Use what you know about root words and suffixes to help you figure out the meaning of an unfamiliar word.

Splashy Endings

Draw a line to match each word to its meaning.

1. careless   full of hope

2. hopeful   full of care

3. careful   without hope

4. hopeless   without care

Circle the suffix in the underlined word. Then write the meaning of the word.

5. Joanne is <u>fearless</u> when she boldly dives into a pool.

_____

6. It is <u>painful</u> when Hector does a belly flop.

_____

Building Essential Language Arts Skills: Grade 3 © Scholastic Inc.

Name: _____ Date: _____

Putting Down Roots

Circle the word that has the same root as the bold word. Underline the common root.

1. reality   realize   relate

2. bicycle   motorcycle   pickle

3. active   forgive   action

4. prevent   paper   invention

5. final   fishy   finish

6. unfortunately   fortune   forty

7. beginning   inning   begin

Putting Down Roots (continued)

Copy the words you circled on page 53 in these spaces.
Then use the letters in the boxes to solve the riddle.

1. ☐ __ __ __ __ __ __

2. __ __ __ ☐ __ __ __ __ __

3. __ __ __ __ ☐ __

4. __ __ __ __ __ ☐ __ __ __

5. __ __ __ ☐ __ __ __

6. __ __ __ __ ☐ __

7. __ __ __ ☐ __ __ __

> **Why were the words clapping and shouting?**
>
> They were _____ for their team!

Use the clues to write a new word with the same root.

8. This word has the same root as **bicycle**. It is what you can do with empty bottles.

_____

9. This word has the same root as **active**. It names a person who plays a part in a movie.

_____

Name: _____ Date: _____

A dictionary lists all the meanings of a word.
For example, the word *cool* might mean *chilly, calm, unfriendly,* or *excellent.*

Track Word Meanings

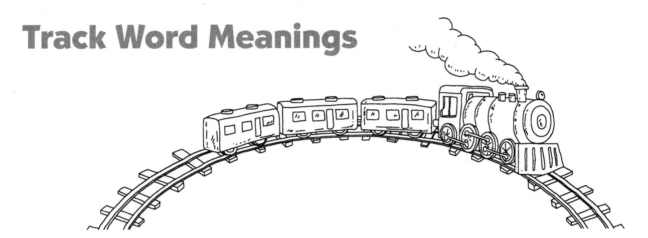

Write two meanings for each word. Use the dictionary if you need help.

1. train _____

_____

2. kind _____

_____

3. mine _____

_____

Choose one word from the box to fill in the blanks in each sentence.

> stable   leaves   scale

4. How much will a fish _____ weigh if you put it on a _____?

5. During the earthquake the horse's _____ was not _____.

6. This bird _____ before the last _____ fall.

Name: _____   Date: _____

Let the Cat Out of the Bag

Read the sentences. Circle the letter that shows the meaning of the idiom.

1.  Nina said that the math homework was <u>a piece of cake</u>.
   a. a yummy dessert
   b. easy to do

2.  Dad asked me to <u>give him a hand</u> after school.
   a. help him do something
   b. cut off part of an arm

3.  Everyone has a cold this week. We're <u>all in the same boat</u>.
   a. sharing the same problem
   b. sailing away in a ship

4.  We're going to <u>hang out</u> in the park after school.
   a. swing by the hands
   b. spend time together

Building Essential Language Arts Skills: Grade 2 © Scholastic Inc.

Name: _____ Date: _____

Use words that help people see, hear, touch, smell, or taste in their mind what you are describing. For example: *The fuzzy yellow chicks chirped softly in their box.*

Using Good Sense

Choose words from the box that describe the objects. Write the words below each picture.

> juicy   sharp   metal   hard   sweet   round

1. _____   4. _____

2. _____   5. _____

3. _____   6. _____

Use the words to write a sentence about each picture.

7. _____

_____

8. _____

_____

Name: _____ Date: _____

 Words that have similar meanings can be different in degree or intensity. For example, *breeze*, *wind*, and *gale* all have similar meanings, but only the last one will knock you down!

Step It Up

The words in each box have different shades of meaning.
Put them in order on the word ladders.

1. (howl   giggle   laugh   grin)

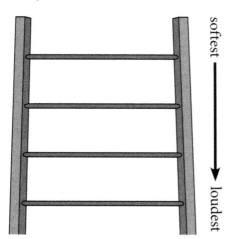

softest ⟶ loudest

2. (jog   sprint   run   walk)

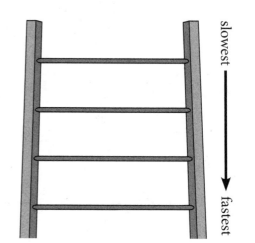

slowest ⟶ fastest

3. (hot   warm   lukewarm   scorching)

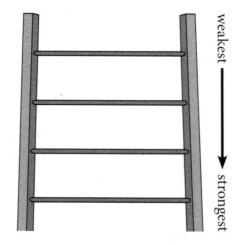

weakest ⟶ strongest

Building Essential Language Arts Skills: Grade 3 © Scholastic Inc.

Name It!

Look at the words with different shades of meaning under each picture.
Fill in the blanks with your own ideas.

Name a food that is:

1. good   _____

2. delicious _____

Name an insect that is:

3. small   _____

4. tiny   _____

Name a place that is:

5. fun   _____

6. thrilling _____

Name an animal that:

7. hops   _____

8. leaps   _____

Name: _____ Date: _____

When and Where?

Jen's Camp Schedule

	Tuesday	Thursday
10:00 – noon	Birdwatching along Barton Creek	Building a bat house at the woodshop
noon – 1:00	Picnic lunch beneath the oak trees	Picnic lunch in the meadow
1:00 – 3:00	Bug races!	Hike to the top of Bald Hill

Use the schedule to answer the questions below.
Answer in complete sentences using the signal words.

1. What will Jen be doing at camp on Thursday after building a bat house?

_____

2. Where will Jen be birdwatching on Tuesday?

_____

3. Where will Jen eat lunch on Tuesday?

_____

Answer Key

page 7
1. thing; bus
2. person; girl
3. place; bakery
4. (Duke) is a big white dog.
5. This dog was elected mayor of (Cormorant.)
6. (Cormorant) is a very small town in (Minnesota.)
7. The town is full of dogs like (Duke,) but only one person lives there.
8. That person is (Dolores Cormorant,) a big dog lover.

page 8
1. foxes, boxes
2. bunches, lunches
3. bushes
4. watches
5. brushes
6. glasses

page 9
1. cowboys
2. keys
3. babies
4. monkeys
5. hobbies
6. puppies
7. berries
8. bunnies

page 10
1. lives
2. loaves
3. wolves
4. cliffs
leaves, scarves, halves

page 11
1. geese
2. women
3. children
4. feet
5. sheep
6. deer
7. cacti
8. teeth

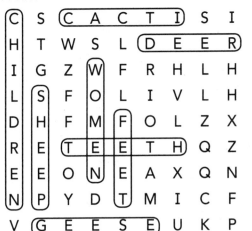

page 12
Concrete Nouns: pencil, president, water, calendar
Abstract Nouns: childhood, freedom, fear, friendship

page 13
1. bear; it
2. Amy; her
3. Kevin; his
4. Our family; we
5. Jon; he
6. Paul and Matt; them

page 14
1. shorts
2. Tony and Frank
3. my brother and I
4. them
5. he
6. it

page 15
1. fell
2. landed
3. was running
4. are chasing
5. is coming
6–8. Responses will vary.

page 16
1. started
2. added, divided
3. subtracted
4. multiplied, ended
5. walked, talked
6. waved
7. played
8. hurried

page 17
1. built
2. went
3. brought
4. drank
5. took
6. ate

page 18
1–4. Sentences will vary.

page 19
1. will happen
2. will eat
3. will wake up
4. will drive
5. will take
6. will get
7. will travel
Stories will vary.

page 20
1. dogs; bark
2. stars; sparkle
3. squirrel; nibbles
4. sun; shines
5. cat; loves
6. Snow and ice; cause
7. leaves; fall

page 21
1. ugly, brown
2. juicy
3. full
4–7. Responses will vary.

page 22
1. nicer
2. more exciting
3. more important
4. happier
5. juicier
6. more difficult
7. rounder
8. more delicious

page 23

1. kindest   2. most beautiful
3. most intelligent   4. funniest
5. most helpful; responses will vary
6. tastiest; responses will vary
7. nicest; responses will vary
8. most interesting; responses will vary

page 24

1. when   2. how   3. where
4. how   5. when   6. where
7. brightly, slowly   8. outside, tomorrow
9–10. Responses will vary.

page 25

1. or   2. but   3. and
4. and   5. or   6. but

page 26

1. my room is messy again.
2. because I left them on the floor.
3. I will put them away.
4. while I clean my room.
5. so I can use it for school tomorrow.
6. I need to clear off my bed.

page 27

1. Pablo Pistachio gave the rat wings, and it looked pleased.
2. Pablo likes butterflies, so he decided to combine one with a fish.
3. Pablo put a turtle's shell on a duck, and he put a duck's bill on a turtle.
4. He could give the raccoon a camel's hump, or he could give it a lion's face.
5. The giraffe looked good with feathers, but the hippo did not.

page 28

1. but   2. so   3. and   4. or
5–6. Sentences will vary.

page 29

Responses will vary. Sample responses:
1. We will eat the birthday cake after we open the presents.
2. I got a stomachache because I ate too much cake.
3. The kids played games before they ate.
4. They took turns whacking the piñata until it burst.
5. We'll go out for pizza when it's time for dinner.
6. We sang in the car while Dad drove us to dinner.

page 30

1–3. Responses should include titles of a book, TV show, and movie.
4. March of the Penguins
5. Casey at the Bat
6. Cloudy with a Chance of Meatballs
7. Tales of a Fourth Grade Nothing

page 31

1. Mr. Jack Frost lives at 1000 Cold Street, Burrville, Alaska.
2. Ms. Anita Mittens lives at 345 Flake Lane, Snowtown, New York.

Mr. Jack Frost
1000 Cold Street
Burrville, Alaska
99501

Ms. Anita Mittens
345 Flake Lane
Snowtown, New York
11901

page 32

1. Paul wants to visit Paris, France.
2. Have you ever been to Cheyenne, Wyoming?
3. We had fun visiting Toronto, Canada, last year.
4. Egon moved here from Budapest, Hungary.
5. Austin, Texas, gets very hot in the summer.
6. San Francisco, California, can be very foggy.

page 33

1. Ms. Taylor said, "I'm your new teacher."
2. Frank said, "I want to read a book about explorers."
3. My sister asked, "What movie do you want to see?"
4. Jim shouted, "Shoot the ball!"
5. "I heard a strange noise," Lisa whispered.
6. Cary mumbled, "I forgot my math homework."
7. "You need to rake the leaves," said Dad.

Building Essential Language Arts Skills: Grade 2 © Scholastic Inc.

page 34
1. Josh said, "I lost my cell phone."
2. Mom asked, "Have you checked your pockets?"
3. "Yes! Of course!" Josh replied.
4. "I'll call you," offered Mom.
5. Josh said, "Well, I might have missed a pocket."
6. "I think I hear something ringing," Mom said.

page 35
1. cat's   2. horse's   3. Tom's
4. school's   5. kitten's   6. toy's
7. turtle's

page 36
1. bees'   2. farmers'   3. cars'
4. students'   5. foxes'   6. chickens'

page 37
1. buried   2. stayed   3. tried
4. hoping   5. covered   6. smiled

page 38

chopped	chopping
flipped	flipping
boiled	boiling
drained	draining
whipped	whipping

Sentences will vary.

page 39
1. knife   2. autumn   3. climb   4. listen
5. wrong   6. sign   7. castle
Answer: A knit wit!

page 40
1. photograph   2. laugh   3. coughing
4. rough   5. effort   6. shelf
7. alphabet

page 41
1. Field   2. ceiling   3. eight
4. height   5. neighbor
6. friendly; cashier

page 42
1. preview   2. impolite   3. dislike
4. rebuild   5. unable

```
C  K  E  I  I  E  U  P  E  T
R  U  W  M  S  J  O  R  K  K
U  N  X  P  G  C  W  E  J  Q
Z  A  K  O  Z  S  H  V  C  V
D  B  L  L  V  W  V  I  A  A
Q  L  K  I  J  N  N  E  N  E
G  E  Z  T  K  H  K  W  D  P
L  S  E  E  T  I  L  D  Z  N
D  I  S  L  I  K  E  A  E  A
U  D  R  E  B  U  I  L  D  R
```

page 43
1. teacher   2. helpful   3. flavorless
4–6. Responses will vary.

page 44
1. deer   2. goat   3. Responses will vary.
4. monkey   5. lion   6. Responses will vary.
7. elephant   8. butterfly   9. Responses will vary.
10. rhinoceros   11. alligator   12. Responses will vary.

page 45
1. ant, candy, kind, nose, tiny
2. laugh, laundry, law, lazy, lead
3. Responses will vary.

page 46
1. dress, drink   2. honey, homonym, honest
3–4. Responses will vary.

page 47
1. Anna cracked some eggs into the <u>sizzling</u> frying pan.
2. She <u>slid</u> them out of the pan and served them to Matt.
3. "Eggs are boring!" Matt <u>complained</u>.
4. "Try this," Anna said, <u>squirting</u> some hot sauce on them.
5. Matt <u>spit</u> the food out of his mouth. "Too hot!" he cried.

page 48

1. spoken	2. written	3. written
4. spoken	5. spoken	6. written

page 49

1. d	2. a
3. d	4. c
5. b	6. b

page 50

1. very bad	2. tiring	3. rested
4. correctly	5. great place	6. very good

page 51

1. prepaid
2. disbelief
3. unacceptable
4. uncertain: not sure
5. disorganized: not orderly
6. preview: to look at ahead of time

page 52

1. without care
2. full of hope
3. full of care
4. without hope
5. fearless; without fear
6. painful; full of pain

page 53

1. realize	2. motorcycle	3. action
4. invention	5. finish	6. fortune
7. begin		

page 54

1. realize	2. motorcycle	3. action
4. invention	5. finish	6. fortune
7. begin		

Answer: They were rooting for their team!

8. recycle	9. actor

page 55

1–3. Responses will vary. Sample responses:
1. A vehicle that runs on tracks
   To get in shape
2. A type
   Nice
3. Something that belongs to me
   A place in the ground where people dig for metals and minerals
4. scale, scale
5. stable, stable
6. leaves, leaves

page 56

1. b	2. a	3. a	4. b

page 57

Order of 1–3 can vary.

1. juicy	2. sweet	3. round

Order of 4–6 can vary.

4. hard	5. sharp	6. metal

7–8. Sentences will vary.

page 58

1. grin	2. walk	3. lukewarm
giggle	jog	warm
laugh	run	hot
howl	sprint	scorching

page 59

Responses will vary.

page 60

1. Jen will have a picnic lunch in the meadow after building a bat house at the woodshop.
2. On Tuesday, Jen will be birdwatching along Barton Creek.
3. On Tuesday, Jen will eat lunch beneath the oak trees.

Building Essential Language Arts Skills: Grade 2 © Scholastic Inc.